A MACDONALD BOOK

First published in Great Britain in 1988
by Macdonald & Company (Publishers) Ltd
London & Sydney
A Pergamon Press plc company

Printed and bound in Spain by Cronion S.A.

Macdonald & Company (Publishers) Ltd
Greater London House
Hampstead Road
London NW1 7QX

British Library Cataloguing in Publication Data
Lewis, Tracey
Oh Pebble! — (Picture Fiction).
I. Title
823′. 914 [J] PZ7

ISBN 0-356-11975-0
ISBN 0-356-11976-9 Pbk

Dep. Leg. B-4959-88

Oh Pebble!

Tracey Lewis

Macdonald

Sarah has a new kitten.
The kitten's name is Pebble.

Pebble likes to climb the curtains,

sharpen his claws on Dad's chair,

and play with Mum's knitting.

Oh Pebble!

Mum looks cross.

Mum makes Pebble play in the garden.

Pebble likes the garden.

There are flowers to lie on,

trees to climb,

birds to watch,

and clothes to swing on.

Oh Pebble!

Mum looks even crosser.

Pebble runs away to hide.

Sarah can't find him anywhere.

'Out of the way, Sarah,' says Dad.
'I must water my tomato plants.'

Pebble is very wet and cold.
He's not going to hide any more.

'Oh Pebble, there you are.'
Sarah takes Pebble to Mum and Dad.
They laugh when they see
how wet he is.

Mum wraps Pebble up
in a big soft towel.
She isn't cross any more.

Soon Pebble is fast asleep.

Everybody loves him really.